W9-DFD-004

Landscape in Britain

LANDSCAPE IN BRITAIN

photographs by Charlie Waite
commentary by Adam Nicolson

THAMES AND HUDSON

First published in the United States
in 1984 by Thames and Hudson Inc.,
500 Fifth Avenue, New York, New York 10110

Photographs © 1984 Charlie Waite
Text copyright © 1984 Adam Nicolson

Layout: Lawrence Edwards/Judy Dauncey

Library of Congress Catalog Number 84–50007

All rights reserved. No part of this publication
may be reproduced, stored in a retrieval system,
or transmitted, in any form or by any means,
electronic, mechanical, photocopying,
recording or otherwise, without the prior
permision of the copyright holders.

Printed and bound in Italy by New Interlitho

PREVIOUS PAGE: LEFT, ACROSS THE TERNE VALLEY, SHROPSHIRE;
CENTRE, TOWARDS CADER IDRIS, GWYNEDD, WALES;
RIGHT, FIELD OF OILSEED RAPE, NETTLESTEAD, KENT

I heard a thousand blended notes,
While in a grove I sate reclined,
In that sweet mood when pleasant thoughts
Bring sad thoughts to the mind.

To her fair works did Nature link
The human soul that through me ran;
And much it grieved my heart to think
What man has made of man.

William Wordsworth,
from 'Lines Written in Early Spring'

Preface

MARSHWOOD VALE, DORSET

William and Dorothy Wordsworth lived at nearby Pilsden Hill for a time. Dorothy in particular loved this view, and it was said to be 'dearest to her recollection upon the whole surface of the island'.

I have often wondered what induces me to stop at a particular place and to realise that it is a photograph. To explain why seems, oddly enough, both difficult and banal: a desire to please; a feeling for the closeness of the perfect and the decayed in the landscape; an appreciation of how the earth's surface relates to and is influenced by the sky above it; above all a sense of purity. All these, inevitably, are approximations. I want to say that in a photograph I look for an objective equivalent of what I know to be true. When the photograph is right – and there is rarely any uncertainty about that – I feel a glorious sense of completeness with it. Indeed, it is a sort of union.

When the photograph is finally done, I feel a sense of loss. I am always reluctant to leave and the separation is like saying goodbye to an old friend. The relationship has never been very long – a matter of hours at the most – but always remarkably intense. When by chance I have passed one of these many places again, they have seemed strangely distant to me and I would never dream of stopping once more.

It's as though the place had shown itself at its best the first time and will never again recover that perfection.

None of these photographs is of a town or a city. Nor, with one exception, is a single human being to be seen in any of them. It is not that I mind people, only that their presence in a landscape seems to trivialise and distort it. To me having a person in a photograph would be as out of place as appearing in it myself. I am looking for a timelessness and a permanence which the human and the urban cannot convey. I have to admit that a simple hill can mean more to me than any cathedral.

Photographers have always debated whether photographs are taken or made. There is no doubt in my own mind that my choice of camera and its square format – unorthodox for landscape photography – influences my choice of subject. In that way, at least, I *make* the photograph. But in other ways there is no doubt it is a question of taking. I am there simply to receive what is on offer and I can experience a sort of greed in front of a beautiful landscape. I spend a long time looking up, somehow placing myself in that particular spot and getting to know all the dimensions of where I stand on the earth. There is always one moment when I and the landscape are ready, like the moment when a piece of blotting paper gently laid on spilt ink suddenly absorbs all the pattern of ink beneath it. It is then that the photograph is taken and made.

But this has another side to it, and that is the guilt of not contributing to what I have had the good fortune to discover and enjoy. Occasionally it seems to be a vulture existence – arriving, picking up and taking, participating even less than the farmer or the shepherd in the making of these great permanences. All that I can do is plug myself into the current, living for a short time on its power, unrushed and unconcerned. When the connection is made, no questions need to be asked and no answers required. The camera itself becomes no more than a channel along which I and the landscape can pass, for a short time joined up and communicating. It is then that the clarity evolves and a sense of peace prevails.

THE SEVEN SISTERS, SUSSEX

Charlie Waite

8

RIVER ITCHEN, MARTYR WORTHY,
HAMPSHIRE

Introduction

There are few stories as powerful as the Greek myth of Antaeus, an African giant who bestrode the heroic mythological landscape of Libya. Any stranger passing through his domain would be forced to wrestle with him. None of his opponents realised that whenever Antaeus was thrown in the fight and touched his mother, the earth, he would draw fresh strength from her and inevitably defeat them. Hercules alone learnt the source of Antaeus' power, and when faced with the invincible giant, picked him up in an enormous bear-hug, lifting him away from the earth he needed, crushing the life out of him, elevated, powerless, in mid-air.

Ripples of meaning spread out from this ancient story about the landscape and our need to stay close to it. Like the best of myths it cannot be explained entirely, nor put into other words. Like the landscape itself, it remains a pattern we can all succumb to, a base-line to be touched like a partner in tag.

I have spent many hours with Charlie Waite collecting photographs for this book. Although a mere

THE THAMES IN FLOOD
WALLINGFORD, OXFORDSHIRE

WOODS NEAR AVENING,
GLOUCESTERSHIRE

RIVER BET, NEAR GRASMERE,
CUMBRIA

NEAR GOLITHA FALLS, RIVER FOWEY,
CORNWALL

*Just beyond this tranquil avenue of
beeches the River Fowey, after a
gentle passage, descends in a series of
turbulent falls towards the sea.*

six feet two inches tall and with a more than human
mother, he is the person who comes nearest to Antaeus
that I know. He never looks for photographs in the
landscape. There is nothing so conscious or purposeful
about it. From some microscopic chinks in the corners
of his eyes he is able to find these perfect images in the
middle of a conversation, or while telling a joke. This
too is something that cannot be explained, a kind of
innate pre-knowledge of 'the radiance consorting with
the dance', as one American poet has described it.
Although he will shudder at the word, there is a sort
of humility in this gift. Like the lens of the camera
itself, the photographer's mind – his mind's eye – must
be all receptivity, a clean, careful funnel for the
landscape's casual juxtapositions and chance
arrangements. But that alone would not be enough;
there is an alertness there too, a sudden snap ability to
home in, frame up and 'make' the picture, as he says.
It is these two contradictory qualities – an easiness and
an appetite, a humility and an ambition – somehow
held together without destroying each other, which
have made the photographs in this book.

The failure to see such moments is perfectly
described by R. S. Thomas in a poem called 'The
Bright Field':

I have seen the sun break through
to illuminate a small field
for a while, and gone my way
and forgotten it. But that was the pearl
of great price, the one field that had
the treasure in it. I realize now
that I must give all that I have
to possess it. Life is not hurrying

on to a receding future, nor hankering after
an imagined past. It is the turning
aside like Moses to the miracle
of the lit bush, to a brightness
that seemed as transitory as your youth
once, but is the eternity that awaits you.

NEAR DOWNHAM MARKET, NORFOLK

PORTESHAM, DORSET

Bare ploughed fields where the chalk dilutes the earth from rich browns to milky cream.

LODDINGTON NEAR UPPINGHAM, LEICESTERSHIRE

An increasingly rare sight, as the rounded bales take over from the haystacks all over the countryside.

NEAR MELROSE, THE BORDERS, SCOTLAND

Of course, Charlie is tapping a shared resource. His way of knowing is only a heightened version of what we all know. But here too there is a sort of contradiction. I have in my own mind, and anyone who looks through this book will soon gather, the idea of a 'Charlie Waite Photograph'. There is a slightly rotten shed in the middle distance. The sky unfurls in motorway diagrams of receding cumulus, wisping at the edges. The country has been entirely cleared of human beings, and almost nothing has happened in it since about 1760. Nothing blurs, and an electric neon-lit clarity hovers over the entire scene. There is a sense of perfection on the verge of decay. It is impossible to call Charlie either a romantic or a classical photographer, since he finds in the most romantic of subjects the classic elements of balance, measured near-symmetry and the comfort of patterned order.

His landscape only rarely responds. It is usually as still as the photograph itself, making for a plu-perfect stillness, a stilled stillness in the picture itself. I think this is part of the reason for the intensity of these images. When the landscape does answer back, the effect is odd, slightly ludicrous. Look, on page 76, at the sheep on Gospel Pass, peering, inquisitive, momentarily individual (lured on, I can reveal, by a slice of Mother's Pride bread) and she becomes a faintly absurd participant in the landscape, a nearly-articulate intelligence in the wrong world. And here you can realise the essential quality of these photographs, of this vision of the landscapes of Britain. It is a remade world, almost a vision of another, purer planet, in which the most ordinary elements appear highlit, intensely concrete, both familiar and strange, both universal and peculiarly Charlie's at the same time.

There is nothing grandiose about this way of looking at the landscape. It makes its choices. It is rigorously exclusive of what will not fit. (There have been numberless occasions when I have implored Charlie to photograph eminently picturesque scenes and have been quietly told not to interfere.) But the reasons for inclusion or exclusion are more to do with the arrangement of elements on the ground-glass

NEAR PLUMPTON, SUSSEX

20

FALLING FOSS
NEAR LITTLE BECK, YORKSHIRE

The compulsion to throw in a coin here was
irresistible, as was the compulsion to stay.

screen than the romance of the subject matter. He does not need the 'big bow-wow', as Jane Austen described Walter Scott's plots and characters. His is an Antaean need for the intimate integrity of the landscape's details. 'I cannot be weaned/off the earth's long contour, her river-veins,' as Seamus Heaney has written. It is the bright field, the lit bush, the specific universal. He may now and then be:

. . . drawn to promontories where the sea
Is grey and intemperate, with sheer juts
Of rock into rapacious, upheaved waters . . .

in the words of Alan Brownjohn's poem 'Near Gun Hill', but closer to the centre of Charlie Waite's photography is the ability:

. . . to feel suddenly how the huge chords
Don't dramatise themselves, don't flaunt themselves
In obvious frenzies here, but lie and wait
While the first creature of the swarm climbs slowly
Unsheathing a black wing and tilts one reed.

Adam Nicolson

OVERLEAF: RIVER CUCKMERE BETWEEN SEAFORD AND EASTDEAN, SUSSEX

Landscape in Britain

NEAR SWINSTEAD, LEICESTERSHIRE

There is no great width in the landscape of Britain. The country is too narrow. It is cabinned inside its coasts, and, inland the horizon is never formed by the curvature of the earth alone. The British landscape exists within tight limits and there is none of that continental or oceanic sense of infinite regression over the horizon, where the clouds and their landscape bend downwards and out of sight like the disappearing repetitions of two mirrors. Whenever some scheme is laid to smooth out the landscape and plane off its awkwardness, like a new reservoir or the removal of hedges, it runs foul of the deep national affection for the knobbly interruptedness of the country.

Even to talk about the 'British landscape' in the singular runs against this feeling for its particularities. For some reason the idea of 'Britain' is too much of an abstraction to be associated with one mental landscape. Each of the words 'England', 'Scotland' and 'Wales' summons an instant – if approximate – mind-view, but 'Britain' is too political for such an image. There could never be a football team called 'Britain' which

ORCHARD AT PADDOCK WOOD, KENT

*The fine management of an English orchard is
amply rewarded – not only in the autumn.*

WEST KINGSDOWN, KENT

*Old Man's Beard in November is surprisingly
active, and threatens to overwhelm its neighbours.*

wasn't an artificial conglomeration, and the same is true of the landscape. But the categories are never clear and as George Mikes wrote in *How to Be an Alien*, 'When people say England, they sometimes mean Great Britain, sometimes the United Kingdom, sometimes the British Isles – but never England.' These pages, I am afraid, will be no exception.

Local allegiance of course lags behind the technology. Britain is actually more integrated than almost any other country. Over the past two hundred years canals, roads, railways, national newspapers, the post, radio and television, the electric grid and above all motorways and cars have effectively made the local unimportant. It does not matter if a television programme comes from Bristol or Birmingham, or if clothes are made in Glasgow or Gillingham. It is now an immensely mobile country, where Bristol is only five hours driving from the Scottish Highlands and a family from Birmingham can spend the weekend in Devon. We may be reaching the stage where the place we live in the country, the regional landscape we can think of as our own, has no more meaning than the place we live in the village or the street. Being near a shop in Leicestershire and near a shop in Kent may become more similar than not being near a shop in either.

But there is a strong counter-current, remembered from a previous England. When William Cobbett was making his journeys, recorded in *Rural Rides* in the early nineteenth century, he met a woman in Sussex who had never been to the village four miles from her own, and did not know the way there. This pre-pre-industrial rootedness is still a powerful force underlying the general attitude to the landscape. In the less inspected areas of the mind England is still a nest of separate places, with definite identities and boundaries but folded in with each other to make the whole. Great attention is now paid to the materials of which villages and towns are made. Each county will have its slightly different style of nameplate for the entrances to villages. There is a desire, which is perhaps nostalgic or perhaps unconsciously aesthetic, to have the whole country composed of identifiable and related parts. We

HAWTHORN TREES NEAR KETTLESHUME, CHESHIRE

CROWHOLE BOTTOM
NEAR WANTAGE, BERKSHIRE

CAMEL ESTUARY, NORTH CORNWALL

*The lifeboat coxwain across the estuary assured
me that the sands never repeat themselves in shape,
in a landscape of constantly shifting perspective.
Behind me lies the church of St Enedoc.*

TOWARDS ABBOTSBURY CHAPEL
AND CHESIL BEACH, DORSET

do not want the single unbroken monotone but instead that strange hybrid state (as we must imagine it was) where Shropshire is Shropshire, but also England, and where England is always one country, but never quite the same version of that country.

This same mythological Britain floats many hundreds of miles off the European mainland in a world of its own. When the English think of their relationship to Europe, they think of Hastings, Agincourt, Blenheim and Dunkirk, not the channel tunnel or the twenty-two miles between Dover and Calais. They ignore the fact that the cross on top of St Paul's Cathedral would stick out of the water if the whole building were placed in the deepest part of the Straits of Dover. Actually swimming the Channel is seen as a Herculean denial of 'The Way Things Are'. Unlike the Romans, the Russians, the Turks, the French, the Spanish, the Swedes, the Austrians and the Germans, the English have never really entertained the idea of an empire on the continent of Europe. Membership of the Common Market has been treated in the Agincourt-raiding-party style of diplomacy, to the dismay of the other Europeans whose history is one of attachment and deep involvement in the main body of European affairs.

But the England that results from insularity and an intense idea of itself is not a remote place, not on the edge of any continent or stuck out from the landmass into the ocean. It is in the middle, the world's navel, independent of anywhere else. It is warm but never scalding, an indolent day in late June about thirty years ago. A light wind blows other smells in from across a small valley and the background is an intermittent insect hum. There is shadow and warmth. It is a field beside a wood where trees spread narrowing branches out over the grasses. There is no longer any need of a haycart or a shepherd to complete this ancient scene. It is now a place we may have been to once or twice before, a reconstituted memory, a cider picnic where you shut your eyes and stretch. The hedges are thick and unfocused, full of dog-roses. There are no strangers in the party and some of the children are very young. It is the present perfect, the time in which

BLACKTHORN TREE IN FULL BLOOM
ST CLERE, KENT

BETWEEN HORNER AND PORLOCK, SOMERSET

NEAR JEDBURGH, THE BORDERS, SCOTLAND

no change occurs. The breeze lifts the shirts a little and we feel it between the cotton and our skin. At the bottom of the field there is a river where we paddle. The grasses on the bank brush against our calves. The stream floor is gravelly and is blotted with sunshine like the side of a fish. Bunches of grass, torn up and thrown in, float easily away. We nibble sweet stubs of grass between our front teeth. We have never known a day like it and have never loved ourselves more. We eat early cherries and have mayonnaise with most things. We already feel sad.

The dream place is a field. No word in the language is more soaked in association – battles, heraldry and games on one side, Housman-Hardy England on the other. The word originally meant no more than the open space not covered by the forest, but that meaning – with the landscape that created it – has now disappeared. The field is enclosed, shut off from its neighbours but dependent on them, all of them part of a continuous pattern. Lowland England consists of this divided continuity. Only after you have seen the monotonous endlessness of the northern European plain, where the blocks of birch and pine forest are the only interruptions to the razored emptiness, and where farms, to an English eye, have been arbitrarily dropped on the surface of a billiard earth, can you thank God for the hedges of England and all their mild, semi-permeable divisiveness.

The English may need to exaggerate their differences. The hills are only the worn-down stumps of old mountains, most of them the outer ripples of the great continental ranges, now grassy and rounded over. But as W. H. Auden wrote:

So long as there's a hill ridge somewhere
The dreamer can place his land of Marvels.

Indeed, you only have to compare a picture by Samuel Palmer with the real chalk downs near his house at Shoreham in Kent, to see that his eye, like every Englishman's, needed to inflate them. The modest profiles of the real hills were too gentle for the laden meanings he wanted them to bear.

ABOVE BOLTBY, NORTH YORKSHIRE

CLIPSHAM, NEAR STAMFORD,
LEICESTERSHIRE

*I questioned the farmer about this one tree, so
carefully left to stand alone; he told me that it
hadn't yet finished living.*

SILVER WILLOWS, NEAR ISLIP,
CAMBRIDGESHIRE

NEAR WREXHAM, CLYWD, WALES

NEAR MOULSFORD, BERKSHIRE

Hedges and walls do in the real landscape what Palmer's exaggerations did in his pictures: they intensify the individuality of each place. Whether you walk through the tiny snakeskin network of prehistoric fields and lanes in Devon and Cornwall, where the sheer bulk and weight of stones in the walls have guaranteed their permanence; or in the chestnut and oak-edged fields of Kent, where woods and streams are the natural divisions and the thick, bulbous hedges only a footnote; or in the perfect mattress pastures of Leicestershire and Rutland, the best hunting country in Europe, where the Enclosure Commissioners of the eighteenth and nineteenth centuries drew out their grid of fields, now marked by low thorn hedges, shaped each winter into smooth rounded tubes for jumping, like the piping along the edges of sofas; or even in the Fens, where at first sight there is no division at all in the glutinous productivity of black earth, but where deep lodes and channels separate places that are only yards apart by many miles; in all these landscapes of England, all in their different dialects and vocabularies, the divisions arrange for the separate particularity of each place, each field named, each one part of the system, each important in itself.

If you keep to the paths through this netted landscape you experience a sort of reassurance, a feeling that you are moving through a network of agreements. It is a mild pattern of consensus. The lowland landscape is an image of civility and a polite division of spoils. Nothing is clearer than where one place ends and another begins. And even if on the ground there is no indication of who owns what, the neatness of the division and its visible embodiment in the hedges and walls will reassure you that somewhere these things are known and accepted.

There can be few more seductive representations of this agreed landscape than the modern maps of the Ordnance Survey. They occupy a niche halfway between a picture and a book. We 'read' them but there is nothing consecutive or line by line about the way we learn what they mean. In a map, a landscape, and a picture, the mind wanders in and out of the

NEVERN CHURCHYARD,
PEMBROKESHIRE, WALES

45

OAK TREE, NEAR TUGBY, LEICESTERSHIRE

SPINNEY AT SOUTH ARRETON, ISLE OF WIGHT

The ivy here is remarkably deep, and so vibrantly alive it's hard to see it as the harbinger of destruction.

woods, somehow simultaneously in many parts of it, gathering information like a crystal hung in solution, silently accreting in sympathy with the environment, adopting and converting what it finds to hand. Cleaned of the unnecessary noise with which a real landscape is filled, a map is above all intelligible. It reduces the variety of things to a simple code, expressed in the key, where a green block is a wood whatever its trees and a town is a town is a town.

This easy knowledge of a place in its maps can lead to strange experiences. The first time I ever went to the chalk downs in Wiltshire, where the earth is thicker with the past than anywhere else in the country, it was the winter. I had spent long hours in London looking at the maps, where the grey nipples of the barrows and the long scar of the Wansdyke, all of them with their Gothic script and declared antiquity, were more important than the pattern of the contours and the arrangement of new roads. I arrived there alone at night, with the map complete in my head. The following morning, in what must have been a state of severe disturbance, I set out into the map landscape I knew too well. It was like going to Russia and finding all my prejudices confirmed. I could tick off the repetitions of the propaganda one after another in the streets and not know if what I was seeing existed out there or was half inside me, the imposition of a loaded brain. Wiltshire, in a strange reversal, became the product of the map, my map, and as I walked over the downland and the old mounds and grooves on its surfaces, it seemed as if I were creating the landscape around me. I was sculpting it by looking at it. I only had to imagine something and it would exist.

Everywhere the pattern fell out as I knew it would. At the end of the day I arrived near Avebury, at Silbury Hill, the huge neolithic puddling bowl of chalk and turf.

A few hundred yards away was the source of the River Kennet in a tiny chalk bowl, about five feet across, naturally cut into the terrace of the field above it. The small spring had frozen. It had oozed out and accumulated as a stalactite fist of ice, opaquely white, halfway up the small chalk cliff behind it. Around it,

THE COVE AT AVEBURY, WILTSHIRE

49

NEAR STONEHENGE, WILTSHIRE

CHIRK CASTLE, CLWYD, WALES

The absurdly ideal light for such a castle magnifies its formidable presence against the brilliant backdrop of a vivid sky.

on the floor of the small theatre where the river began, someone had laid hundreds of cut snowdrops. They had been bought in a shop, three or four hundred of them, in bunches that were held together with elastic bands. Whoever had come here in this half-primitive, half-consciously modern act of worship had undone most of the bunches and laid them out below the frozen spring, leaving the others still held together in their elastic bands. I did not touch them. But the sight destroyed the reverie of map-induced creation which had returned to me in pulses throughout the day. One sharp blow is all that is needed to impose the real landscape on the solipsistic map. No elastic bands and no snowdrops appeared on the Ordnance Survey. They were no part of the National Grid. They were too odd and too transient. They showed that the map is an abstraction, even a distortion. In its own way it is a sort of pastoral, a perfect stilled world in which unchanging elements interlock without difficulty.

Only half a million people, about three per cent of the working population, now gain their living from the land. The rest of the people are urban, a population at the other end of a long swing that began with the commercial and urban revolution of the twelfth century. Before that sudden burst of inventiveness and energy, three per cent of a much smaller population lived in towns and cities, the rest in the fields. Most now are strangers to the country, inevitably treating it as an aesthetic object intended for visual pleasure. In lowland Britain it is the detail of care and the patina of continued use that makes it beautiful for us. It is now thought to be a functional sort of beauty, unconsciously emerging from the uses for which it is intended, without – except in the case of great houses and their estates – the intervention of conscious design. 'Hand-made' the landscape historians call it, referring us to John Ruskin's idea of the workman half-consciously creating beauty with his hands in a direct transference of quality from his soul to the object he makes.

This modern sense of functional beauty in the rural landscape has been taken over, oddly enough, from a previous idea of the beauty of cities. At the time of the

THE NEW FOREST
NEAR WILVERLEY, HAMPSHIRE

LAMMERMUIR, NEAR DUNS, THE BORDERS,
SCOTLAND

*It was a long wait for the arrival of the solitary
cloud to soften the harshness of the midday sun.*

FARNDALE, YORKSHIRE

BESIDE THE FOSSE WAY, GLOUCESTERSHIRE

SAND DUNES ON THE CAMEL ESTUARY AT ROCK, CORNWALL

THE HARBOUR AT CHARLESTON, CORNWALL

The harbour walls look impregnable, but sadly Charleston harbour is now almost unused.

THE MANGER, AT UFFINGTON, BERKSHIRE

OVERLEAF: PETWORTH PARK, SUSSEX

Somehow the deer themselves seemed proud and privileged to roam in the grounds of one of Britain's finest estates.

Renaissance, it was the city that represented in men's minds the place where the landscape was best organised. In the city the various habits and occupations of men interlocked exactly, making a seamless pattern of wealth and well-being. Heaven itself was conceived of as a city. In the Middle Ages the worldliness (or economic efficiency) of urban life drove the religious to escape to the wilderness, to build their monasteries in remote places, but it was an escape from the systematic to the non-systematic, the mirror image of the reasons for which people desert the cities today. (London lost ten per cent of its population between 1971 and 1981, Manchester seventeen per cent, Liverpool sixteen per cent.) The city has now taken over the previous image of the rural landscape, where large quasi-natural forces and half-wildernesses verge on the edge of chaos, and where individual wills can have little effect on the way in which the world turns.

Until late in the seventeenth century the city and the garden were grouped together in people's minds and held apart from the countryside. Both city and garden were – in theory at least – walled off, neat and organised places, where rational control of the landscape produced alleys and squares. The country was random by comparison. But over the following century and a half, in a great change of sensibilities that overcame Britain and Europe, the three elements of the city, the garden and the countryside altered their relationship to each other, revolving into the pattern which they hold today. The garden, under the influence of painting, moved away from its more obvious artificialities. It abandoned the enclosing wall, which had been almost the definition of a garden, and buried it as a ha-ha. At the same time the great open fields and commons of England began to be enclosed in stock-proof thorn hedges and stone walls.

There were obvious economic advantages to enclosure – a higher stocking rate and more thorough manuring of fields; the economies of scale; a more effective rotation and less frequent need for fallows; wind protection for crops and stock; less journey time between house and work for both animals and men –

but there was a very important aesthetic side to it too. Allowing nature into the garden allowed the garden into nature, while the new visible divisions of the landscape, its new precision, and the gradual concentration of the land in the hands of fewer and fewer landowners blurred the distinction even further. Many parts of the country came to be made up of large garden-like estates, dotted with the standard hedgerow trees and divided into regular plots, centred on the great house and estate-like garden at its core.

The extraordinary continuity of farmed landscape, garden and city that existed in the eighteenth century, all of them sharing the same presumptions, the same sense of scale, disintegrated with the Industrial Revolution. The city lost all the associations of carefulness. It became a symbol of the failure, or at least the high cost, of human enterprise, rather than its highest achievement. For people like Ruskin, the separation from other landscapes which modern urban life involved represented the worst of the new industrial culture. He campaigned for 'a clean busy street within, and the open country without, with a belt of beautiful garden and orchard round the walls, so that from any part of the city perfectly fresh air and grass, and sight of far horizon, might be reachable in a few minutes walk.' He was not listened to at the time. As Dr Johnson had said: 'It is being concentrated which produces high convenience', and economic convenience remained the decisive factor in urban planning. The result was the notorious and noxious hells that shut their occupants off from anything but repetitions of the immediate nastiness. An anonymous music-hall song from the very end of the nineteenth century makes bitter jokes about a London slum completely shut in by bricks and mortar:

If you saw my little backyard, 'What a pretty spot' you'd
say —
It's a picture on a summer day,
With the turnip tops and cabbages that people don't buy
I make it on a Sunday look all gay.
The neighbours think I grow 'em, and you'd fancy you're in
Kent,

SWEET CHESTNUT IN CLAREMONT PARK,
ESHER, SURREY

65

LONG SUTTON, THE FENS, LINCOLNSHIRE

*An extraordinary consequence of stubble burning. The
farmer told me he had never seen anything like it in forty years.*

NEAR COLYTON, DEVON

Or at Epsom if you gaze into the mews;
It's a wonder as the landlord doesn't want to raise the rent,
Because we've got such nobby distant views.
Oh it really is a very pretty garden,
And Chingford to the eastward could be seen;
With a ladder and some glasses
You could see to Hackney Marshes
If it wasn't for the houses in between.

The real countryside became quite separate. Left alone with all the attributes of the garden, it came to be regarded with nostalgia and all the allure of a paradise lost.

This nostalgia-laden view of the rural landscape came to dominate English attitudes for a century and a half. In 1955 it was joined by another. The date is so precise because in that year Professor W. G. Hoskins published a book called *The Making of the English Landscape*. It was a wholly original book, treating the landscape as evidence for its own history. Professor Hoskins praised those geologists who had dealt with the structure underlying the landscape, 'for they are concerned with facts and are not given to the sentimental and formless slush which afflicts so many books concerned only with superficial appearances.'

It is quite on accusation. Whenever we have thought a landscape beautiful, it suggests, or have suddenly longed in a London street for some remote, empty place, or whenever a poet has written about the spirit of a place, he and we have been neglecting *facts* and have succumbed to sentimental and formless slush. There is a great head of energy stored up behind this materialist attitude to the landscape. It is the spectacle of analytic science, with all its assumptions of the primacy of material things, taking over and colonising, with a great romping delight, a whole area of country that had been the preserve of myth. It is unstoppable within its own logic and can demolish all the easy presumptions: there was less woodland in the Bronze Age than in the eleventh century AD; there was a massive death of the elms in England in about 3700 BC, and the recent decimation is no cause for worry – they will return; there is no wild place in Britain, even the

CLIFF AT ST BEES HEAD, CUMBRIA

NEAR STACKPOLE QUAY, PEMBROKESHIRE

WESTON MOUTH, DEVON

BRAMSHILL FOREST
NEAR FINCHAMPSTEAD, SURREY

*My daughter, who was with me the day I was
here, refused to venture deeper into the trees to
find fircones. A strange and awesome
atmosphere could be felt strongly.*

QUARTZ OUTCROP IN SNOWDONIA, WALES

BLAKENEY, NORFOLK

NEAR TREEN, LANDS END, CORNWALL

WHITEADDER RESERVOIR, ISLE OF SKYE

ST BRIDES BAY, PEMBROKESHIRE COAST, WALES

The one concession to humanity in these photographs, which can cause a sudden shift in judging the scale of the foreground.

remotest moors have been shaped by men or their animals; Great Gable is not an untouched fragment of divine creation – sheep keep it smooth, men landscape it by abstention.

In the materialist view, appearance is superficial. What is important lies hidden, accessible only to the investigating intellect. The metaphor that lies behind such assumptions is archaeology, or perhaps even Freudian psychology. The surface shows nothing. It is only the grass of the field, the obvious present. The interesting and the important are underneath, the further underneath the more important, the older the better.

This habit of thought leads to a circular and paradoxical effect. Dismissing the non-factual as sentimental slush and elevating History as the supreme fact, Professor Hoskins becomes very sentimental about the effect of the present on the appearance of the landscape. 'Since the year 1914,' he writes in his final chapter, 'every single change in the English landscape has either uglified it or destroyed its meaning or both.' Having treated the landscape throughout its history as something composed only of facts, he treats it in his own day as an aesthetic ensemble for which change is destruction. It becomes a painting by Constable or Gainsborough across which 'aeroplanes lay trails like filthy slugs'. For the materialist, the world consists either of facts or slush. If he turns from one, he must wallow in the other. Conceiving of one creates the other. There is no synthesis here, no intuition that the present is of a piece with the past. The coherent look of the rural landscape has deceived him. It looks like a work of art, but the coherence is the result of the people obeying simple guidelines which can be understood and followed by anyone. Not only does function make for beauty but an awareness of beauty, at however humble a level, has always been a prominent fact in the landscape. His contempt for the present-day prevents him from recognising, for example, the gentle modern beauties seen by Philip Larkin's Whitsun couples in a train, who:

GOSPEL PASS, BLACK MOUNTAINS, WALES

THE QUIRANG, ISLE OF SKYE

NEAR SELKIRK, THE BORDERS, SCOTLAND

UPPER SWALEDALE, YORKSHIRE

LANTHWAITE, NEAR GRASMERE, CUMBRIA

Intense shadows on the steeper slopes add drama to some of Britain's remoter uplands – the shadows seem so dense that its sometimes hard to believe that the sun's warmth and light can ever penetrate the deeper cuts.

79

LOCH TUATH, ISLE OF MULL

OVERLEAF: RIVER ETIVE, GLEN ETIVE,
SCOTLAND

*Neither I nor anyone I know has ever seen Glen
Etive, at the head of Glencoe, without its shroud
of vapour.*

*... watched the landscape, sitting side by side
An Odeon went past, a cooling tower,
And someone running up to bowl ...
I thought of London spread out in the sun,
Its postal districts packed like squares of wheat.*

It is sometimes difficult to realise that the appearance
of the landscape is the most important fact about it. It
strikes you first and last, both before and after you
have come to know its history and what it is used for.
And it is easy to forget that the most usual and
hackneyed ideas about the landscape are likely to be
the most powerful because most people believe in
them. A few years ago I met a man in Sussex who
spoke with a Lancashire accent. His story showed how
important the look of a place can be, how it can make
or change a life. In 1932 the slump had hit Bolton in
Lancashire very badly. No one had the prospect of a
steady job. His elder brother had been sacked from a
mill and the next day had taken the train out to
Entwistle, where he drowned himself in a reservoir.
   That was the end of the only job for the family, as
his father was already dead. He looked in the local
paper for jobs. Of the few that were advertised, one
was for apprentice sawyers. He applied and a few days
later received a letter inviting him to come down to
the Duke of Richmond's saw mill at Charlton near
Chichester in Sussex. He made his way down to the
south, walking some of it, hitching lifts for the rest.
When he arrived in the Charlton valley fifty years
before, it was a bright morning with the sun coming
through the corners of the woods and the whole
country filled with a damp freshness like a washed
lettuce. He had never seen anything like it, he said,
nothing so *beautiful*. He had never imagined that such
a beautiful place existed. He became a sawyer (he used
that unused word) married a Sussex girl and lived
there the rest of his life.
   Recently this overriding importance of appearance
in the landscape came nearer to home. My garden wall
fell down, ten yards of it, two feet thick and eight feet
high. I looked out of the window one morning and
saw it collapsed across the public path through the

village. I had always had a respect for wall–builders, especially on the limestone plateaux of the Pennines and on that empty piece of Westmorland between Shap and Kirkby Stephen where tall grey walls divide up acre after acre of grassy fell. The builders, when faced with a stone that fitted in most ways but stuck out a little somewhere else rarely bothered to shape it. This is what I admired: the idea of the wall and its progress over the hillside accommodating and adjusting itself to constant minor fluctuations in the material of which it was made. It was an article of faith with me that only rural genius – something in the blood – could achieve this effect.

I was now to see it all from the other side. The first sign was the exorbitant quotation from Len, the village builder. We surveyed the damage together. He smoked a small cigar and I felt ignorant. He had always lived in the village, but I had been there only a few months. He puffed out the cigar smoke and holding his hand out, palm downwards and fingers outstretched, picked some plaster out of his fingernails. 'It's skilled work,' he said, picking up a bit of half–shattered stone and turning it over, brushing bits of earth away, 'and there's quite a bit of it.' Settled in what we both knew to be the driving seat, he offered me a cigar. 'The stone's a bit flaky. There's a job here.' The interview over, and the relationship between client and patron impossibly confused, I waited for the quotation. It came the next day, typed out on a sort of antique bond in a matching, lined envelope. 'To: clearance of debris, sorting of materials, rebuilding of wall to previous height and width, and other sundries: £1150 + VAT.' Rural genius came very expensive indeed.

I decided to build it myself. Disbelief followed from the neighbours. Surely someone so lacking in rural ancestry could not hope to build a stone wall? Was it wise? Was it *right*? Tactful advice in the corners of the pub. I was to think hard about it, if they were me. It took an eye. Nobody is master of all trades. It did adjoin a public path. Had I considered the insurance angle? Even I began to share the sense of alarm. I was planning to tamper with the rurality of the English

LAKE GREGENEN, GWYNEDD, WALES

85

ST MARY'S LOCH, THE BORDERS, SCOTLAND

landscape – or a small part of it – and the public reaction was as though I had tried to alter the words of 'Hark the Herald Angels Sing'. But once the extra materials had been delivered, the time set aside, the plans laid and, above all, the pride invested, there was no turning back.

I was nervous at the start. I had a friend come to help, or at least to shore me up. I felt fraudulent and unqualified, without that unconscious know-how which I supposed Len and the men in Crosby Ravensworth to have had. But we cleared the collapsed wall and dug the trench for the new foundations. That took two days. Strangers walking past said: 'You've got a job on there' and would say the same thing the following day. I began to realise that sweaty and dirty, we had begun to look like authentic parts of the rural scene. A man who had spent his working life digging wet dirty holes for the Water Board stopped on the path and told us it was a shit life digging holes. People at lunch under the umbrellas of the village pub could regard us all – as I had regarded so many people before – as additions to the scenery they had travelled into the countryside for. Long distance walkers, edging past our barrow and our muck, were either sheepishly silent or brazenly middle class, leaning on their walking-sticks next to our trench like Carlyle and his friend in that famous Victorian painting called '*Work*'.

Once the ground was prepared, we began to rebuild the wall. One always hears – I had always heard – of the wall-builder's miraculous ability to find stones that exactly fit their place in the wall. But this is a fallacy. Nothing is simpler and nothing more obvious. The wall and its stones maintain a constant dialogue. You get to know the unused pile of stones as well as those in the wall you have already used. After the first few hours, everything seems preordained, every stone already in its place. It then becomes a question merely of putting it there. You save some for certain moments and then have a sudden indulgence, a whole course, of good clean squared blocks. You look after the vertical. You use common sense. It is neither sacred nor heavy nor difficult work. Selection of stones is no more a feat

RUINED COTTAGE NEAR TAL–Y–BONT, GWENT, WALES

BUTTERMERE, CUMBRIA

of genius than changing gear in a car.

'Lovely material to work with. So rich,' a Canadian said to me in checked trousers. 'You've done the apprenticeship, I guess.' (I remembered an old man I met in the Cévennes, who was building the walls of a barn. 'They're old stones, aren't they?' I asked him. 'Yes,' he said, 'and they'll probably get a little older.' The acute embarrassment of finding a myth answering back, aware of its being a myth and finding the attitude rather funny.) I saw myself now – the radio on the wall beside me, the sweat-stained shirt, the overall dirt – inside the skin of my own delusions. In the Canadian's shoes – or trousers – I might easily have said 'Lovely material to work with.' Neither of us would have said it to a brickie in south London.

In southern China, in the ninth century AD, one of the great, but now anonymous, masters of the T'ang dynasty painted landscapes of grandeur by first of all getting very drunk indeed. He would then command an orchestra to play the storm passages from contemporary symphonies and after dipping the ends of his long hair into a pool of ink, he would have his assistants spread out long sheets of pure fresh silk. Then, in an ecstasy of laughter, the master – always with a small audience attending – would dance backwards and forwards over his picture, dragging his inky hair after him and smearing at it with the soles of his feet, creating valleys and mountains, crags and boundless smooth plains. 'At the end of the performance,' one of the spectators recorded, 'it seemed as if the sky had cleared after a storm to reveal the true essence of the thousand things.' Later, when all passion was spent, the genius came back to the picture and by adding a bamboo house here and a willow tree there, converted his smeared magnificence into the landscape he had always known it to be. It must be said that contemporary critics, dividing painters into three classes – the competent, the wonderful and the divine – were unable to find a place for this man in any of them. He occupied – with a few other like-minded activists – a class of his own, the 'unconfined' or 'untrammelled'.

ON THE BANKS OF THE RIVER TWEED NEAR ST BOSWELLS, THE BORDERS SCOTLAND

93

ACROSS LOCH TUATH, ISLE OF MULL

NEAR DURNESS, SUTHERLAND, SCOTLAND

GRASMERE, CUMBRIA

Good fortune offered the hill above; on arrival here it was concealed by mist and even the moorhens were still asleep.

PLYNLIMON, DYFED, WALES

BETWEEN DARTMEET AND TWO BRIDGES,
DARTMOOR, CORNWALL

STOODLEY PIKE, THE PENNINES, NEAR
TODMORDON, YORKSHIRE

It is difficult to imagine today such free spirits taking an interest in the landscape. The idea of the landscape has settled into a safer niche in the modern mind, conservative and conservationist, more interested in the historical aspects of it than the sublime. We have, in a way, had too much of the landscape in the past two or three centuries to feel bright, rich or deep about it. The wonderfully funny and imaginative plan to cut an outline figure of Marilyn Monroe, her skirts blown upwards in an image from *The Seven Year Itch*, on the side of a down in Dorset has run foul of local objections. The scheme is to make her outline in chalk opposite the venerable figure of the Cerne Abbas Giant, a prehistoric totem with whose enormous masculinity the villagers are quite willing to cohabit. The difficulty is that Marilyn is still sexy, while the giant is merely historical. His erection is now safely embedded in the cultural humus, blunted and muffled by the rich depth of landscape history with which Dorset and the rest of lowland Britain is coated.

But in the early nineteenth century love of wilderness and of the sublime in landscape was a truly radical gesture. All the Romantic poets, from Blake through Coleridge and Wordsworth to Keats, Shelley and Byron, at least began as political radicals. Blake's poem 'Jerusalem', now sung at Conservative party conferences, the ends of term, society weddings and meetings of the Women's Institute, is an appeal to revolution and to the deeply subversive and disturbing spiritual forces present in the untrammelled English landscape. When Blake wrote: 'I shall not cease from mental fight, nor shall my sword sleep in my hand, Till we have built Jerusalem in England's green and pleasant land' he meant, in flatter English: 'Until I have brought about a complete revolution, and destroyed the industrial system, I will continue to fight with both propaganda and rifles.' It is an extraordinary example of the Establishment's capacity for adoption that members of a Conservative government can sing this battle-hymn as their own.

Like Blake, the young Wordsworth's love of the English landscape was uncompromising, and combined

HOUND TOR NEAR MANATON, DARTMOOR, DEVON

NEAR ST ANNE'S HEAD,
PEMBROKESHIRE, WALES

THE CUILLIN HILLS FROM ELGOL
ISLE OF SKYE

*Standing stones have great significance all over the world,
but never more so than when they stand alone.*

with equally radical political views. His own subversion did not only consist in a sympathy with and a championing of the very poor and rootless, but in a complete abstention from the prevailing social and economic view of the landscape. Dr Johnson had believed that a landscape was beautiful to the degree that it demonstrated the civility of the system that made it. Wild places were worth seeing only so that one could compare them with more prosperous scenes, and reflect on the fragility of human life and human happiness.

Wordsworth, as the culmination of a long movement in European thought, turned this on its head. When he set out for his first walking tour from Cambridge in 1790 he kept it secret from his family and the college authorities in case they thought it so mad or impracticable that they would veto his plans. The attraction of wild places was their apartness from people and not their demonstration of human abilities and failings. The high ground, empty of course for climatic and economic reasons, was where the soul could range without hindrance, where a man could walk naked on a naked earth and learn from it. So close at hand was the sublime for Wordsworth and so immense a moral force that at moments of crisis or ecstasy he used to put his arms around a boulder or the trunk of a tree and hug it, as a stanchion in the flux. The landscape otherwise shed its particularities and from Wasdale or Snowdonia became a universal spectacle in which 'Nature lodg'd the Soul, the Imagination of the whole.' It was then, in:

. . . that serene and blessed mood,
In which the affections gently lead us on –
Until, the breath of this corporeal frame
And even the motion of the human blood
Almost suspended, we are laid asleep
In body, and become a living soul:
While with an eye made quiet by the power
Of harmony, and the deep power of joy,
We see into the life of things.

The contemplative view of nature reached its fullest

REMAINS OF A SAILORS' CHAPEL AT
CWM-YR-EGLWYS, PEMBROKESHIRE, WALES

BRIDGE OF ORCHY, STRATHCLYDE,
SCOTLAND

ABANDONED HOUSE IN THE CHINA CLAY QUARRIES NEAR ST AUSTELL, CORNWALL

DOVEY VALLEY, NEAR MACHYNLLETH,
GWYNEDD, WALES

CAPEL CURIG, SNOWDONIA, WALES

*Though it looks a frozen, silent bleakness, the
wind was blowing gale-force, and knocked me to
the ground.*

and most extreme statement in Wordsworth. The increasing material success of the culture drove him outwards and beyond the mild politeness of the eighteenth century aesthetes. It was at this extreme that the sublime lost touch with the materialist world. It was no longer the ultimate statement of the culture, the point beyond which nothing of relevance could be said, but had actually detached itself from the way in which most people saw the world. Like one of those small balloons of fire that floats away from the tips of the flames, the sublime evaporated into those regions where everything and nothing are indistinguishable. To those who remained rooted in the human landscape of the lowlands and towns, it was no longer a threat, but too absurd to be subversive. As a cultural cipher, it could be adopted, like Blake's 'Jerusalem', by those institutions it was intended to undermine. One of the great ironies is that this very process occurred in the life of Wordsworth himself, who ended his days as a high Tory.

The landscape of Wordsworth's sublime was both created and eventually compromised by the technological achievements of the eighteenth and nineteenth centuries. As both the city and the countryside became fixed in the patterns of human mechanism, freedom of the soul moved upwards on to the moors. 'A wilderness is rich with liberty', Wordsworth wrote, the last word the banner symbol of romanticism. But in the landscape, as in the political history of the nineteenth century, the call for liberty and for the open mountain became part of the bourgeois orthodoxy itself. Love of Great Gable and the Langdale Pikes was twinned to the spread of Manchester and the degradation of Nottingham, and *The Prelude* was stuck to the underside of a Spinning Jenny. Wordsworth, with the ground cut from under him, became acceptable cultural fodder, unsubversive, neutered as an institution like the giant at Cerne Abbas.

> *Am I*
> *To see in the Lake District, then,*
> *Another bourgeois invention like the piano?*

TALY-Y-LLYN AND CADER IDRIS
GWYNEDD, WALES

asked Auden; and then answered:

Well, I won't.

It is a brave denial, but difficult to sustain. Wordsworth's heir today, along with other conservation bodies, is the National Trust. It owns most of the spaces where the great soul roamed, and – like the later Wordsworth himself – it is difficult to think of a more bourgeois institution. Harshly considered, it is an organisation based on a deceit. It preserves large numbers of rural acres in a 'real' version of pastoral. Keith Thomas, the historian of English attitudes to nature, has pointed to the central problem of 'how to reconcile the physical requirements of civilisation with the new feelings and values which that same civilisation has generated.' He goes on: 'Children of today, nourished by a meat diet and protected by a medicine developed by animal experiments, nevertheless take toy lambs to bed and lavish their affection on lambs and ponies. For adults, nature parks and conservation areas serve a function not unlike that which toy animals have for children: they are fantasies which enshrine the values by which society as a whole cannot afford to live.'

It is too painful to regard the Brecon Beacons or the Yorkshire Dales in this way. Reality storms through pastoral like a plague and we do all we can to exclude it. The shops which the National Trust runs on its properties – the chain is among the more successful marketing operations in the country – are concealed in barns and affect a rigorously rural air. Nothing in the National Trust zone can be allowed to challenge belief in its reality. This is the final conquest of the urban mind, the invasion of large parts of the countryside – and wilderness – by a pastoral fiction whose way of thinking is to preserve, to prevent change and half-shamefacedly to show it all to the audience. But no farming system based on Corydon piping love-songs to Amaryllis has ever been viable as an economic unit. Hence the barn-shops, the membership fee, the hidden commercial framework, the smooth urbanity of it all. No blame is to be attached. They are doing it for us.

DESERTED COTTAGE NEAR CARRIGILL, YORKSHIRE

117

HEOL SENNI, BRECON, POWYS, WALES

AFON TYWR, NEAR BRECON, POWYS, WALES

THE FLOORS, NEAR BUDLEIGH SALTERTON, DEVON

119

But you can sympathise with Auden's refusal to see the Lake District as a piano. The landscape is more than its history or the history of attitudes towards it. Nothing is more obvious, yet nothing more difficult to understand. The part-sciences of history and natural history do little but interfere with the vision of the whole. Part of the difficulty may be in the human habit of seeing the landscape divided in two: between the distant and the domestic, the house and the horizon, highland and lowland, radical and conservative, the actual and the sublime, the slush and the facts. This division is not easily dismissed. It is one of the most ingrained of mental patterns. We select one half of the divided reality – the past not the present, the rural not the urban, the natural not the human – and invest it with all the sense of value that really belongs to the undivided whole.

At times in this binary way it has seemed that the only reliable truth appears in the desert or the rocks. There for once the geological reality is free from vegetable crudescence and its chaotic fragility. Only in the great movements of the lithosphere can the important and essential aspects of creation be known. No general principles can be guessed at from the bright fragments of life on the surface, what Hugh MacDiarmid called: 'These foam-bells on the hidden currents of being.'

Where the rock in the landscape emerges, in the high ground or at the coast, the scale of perception changes and the reality of the rock's permanence obliterates any transitory neighbours. It is where the underground stability of the globe shows its colours, formed and frozen in enormous moments of the past. The stone is the ineradicable fact. There are many ruined buildings in the world but no ruined stones. The stone combines in one object the time-scale of the stars and all the presence of a flower. Stones are slow to change; they keep heat and cold in them long after the world around them has moved on.

There is an extraordinary detachment in the world of the rock, an indifference to the motions of the blood and an essential determining ubiquity in the landscape. They are both common-sensical and

SCOTTISH BLACKFACE SHEEP AT LOCHAN LUNN DA BHRA, THE HIGHLANDS, SCOTLAND

STUDELY PARK AT FOUNTAINS ABBEY
NEAR RIPON, YORKSHIRE

TIN MINE, NEAR LYDFORD, DARTMOOR, DEVON

PEN-Y-GHENT, YORKSHIRE

MYNDD PERFEDD, SNOWDONIA, WALES

FARNDALE, YORKSHIRE

sublime, the material for both poetry and for buildings, settled into a certainty from which every other worldly manifestation must take its cue. They make human desires ridiculous, they are the only things without which the world – any world – is inconceivable. They humiliate the scale of human existence and are out of the reach of human understanding. Geologists name them in an an endless taxonomy of irrelevant labels. But even on that relatively banal level, Scotland, where geology was invented, has still resisted complete interpretation. The rocks there have been folded and changed so often that distinguishing their origins and the course of their overlain history is more difficult than identifying the layers in a sheet of pastry that has been rolled, folded and kneaded for hours on the slab. They have a rhythm of growth, destruction and accumulation of their own, which we know but need to ignore, since its scale is not ours. Volcanoes are aberrations, when all that is reliable dissolves itself in a chaos of undoing. But the vents crust over and the rocks regain their calm. That is the image to which we are attracted, that polar strength and constancy to which we turn, from our desperate and interrupted lives, with envy. MacDiarmid wrote:

I am enamoured of the desert at last,
The abode of supreme serenity is necessarily a desert.

In the self-conscious and difficult way of the twentieth century, MacDiarmid is in a line direct from Wordsworth. The stone and its hardness, its inability to compromise, becomes a refuge in the flux of things. It is a reliable base-line where the observer can peg himself down before risking his head in the gales. It rejects the usual idea of safety in the lowlands. For MacDiarmid and many like him the vegetable flux is the landscape of danger.

These are the polarities around which the landscape swings: muddled in with each other and actually inextricable are the two ideas of the landscape as a solid and definite object; and as a place where change is the only constant. Pollution and preservation are

SNOWDONIA, WALES

GARN FARM, THE BLACK MOUNTAINS,
POWYS, WALES

*By coincidence, I found myself here on Christmas Eve,
on my way back home after a lengthy absence.*

entwined in our vision of the landscape. Seen conventionally they could not be further apart. Preservation is the antithesis, the prevention of pollution. Pollution is the destruction which preservation aims to avoid. One is abominated, the other revered. But looked at in another way the opposites suddenly come very close indeed.

The effect of both is to still a process of change. Both impose on the landscape a single element – whether it is mineral or chemical in the case of pollution, cultural or aesthetic in the case of preservation – which stifles the natural development. Pollution interferes with the mechanism of the natural world, the balance between organisms in one biological system; and preservation interferes with the natural mechanism of the human world, which would like to build garages where it is most convenient and turn moorland into money. Both, in their particular zones, bring about one change (the act of stilling) at the expense of the more universal change which they prevent. Both, in effect, look at the landscape with a gorgon's mask, turning their victims to stone. It is conceivable that the whole landscape of Britain will soon consist entirely of the polluted and the preserved. The landscape will then be made up of places as separate and definite as snooker balls, nestled up against each other on the baize, but without the ambiguities and vibrant confusions which have always made the landscape so good a mirror, capable of reflecting every nuance the looker wishes to explore there.

There have always been those like MacDiarmid who have valued permanence and changelessness in the objects around them. But when it comes to the landscape, as Sir Thomas Browne wrote, to hope for permanence is nothing but 'vanity, feeding the wind, and folly.' Galileo, the discoverer of change among the planets, had written in the 1620s: 'I cannot without great wonder hear it being attributed to natural bodies as a great honour and perfection that they are impassible, immutable, inalterable etc . . . It is my opinion that the Earth is very noble and admirable by reason of the many and different alterations, mutations

IN GLEN BRITTLE, ISLE OF SKYE

NEW BEDFORD RIVER OR 'HUNDRED FOOT DRAIN',
NORFOLK

LLYN BRIANNE, NEAR LLANWRTYD WELLS,
POWYS/DYFED BOUNDARY, WALES

and generations which incessantly occur in it. And if, without being subject to any alteration, it had all been one vast heap of sand, or a mass of jade, wherein nothing had ever grown altered or changed, I should have esteemed it a wretched lump of no benefit to the universe, a mass of idleness and in a word superfluous ... If there were as great a scarcity of earth as there is of jewels and precious metals, there would be no king who would not gladly give a heap of diamonds and rubies and many ingots of gold to purchase only so much earth as would suffice to plant a jessamine in a little pot, or to set a tangerine in it, that he might see it sprout, grow up and bring forth such goodly leaves, fragrant flowers and delicate fruit.'

The landscape harbours life in every corner, and the destructive mechanisms of mutation and natural selection are central to it. Ninety per cent of all species that have ever lived are now extinct. Birth depends on the rotting of what has lived. Imagine a landscape in which there is no life, and you must imagine one without growth, the surface of the moon. But imagine another, where there is life but no decay, in which every animal and plant that died remained whole, in above-ground graveyards of pristine corpses, accumulating in stratified perfection. Those bodies would trap all the nutrients on which life depends and for survival all living things would have to cannibalise the mountains of the spotless dead.

Flux is necessary, and, in its sheer proliferation, dependable. There is a sort of comfort in this endless prospect of change. If you turned up the soil of a square yard of an average English field you would find between fifty and eighty thousand seeds in it. Even if some of them had been deprived of light and water since the twelfth century, they would flower as soon as you provided the stimuli. Within a single square mile of Brazilian rainforest you will find three hundred different species of tree. This amazing productivity is achieved at some cost. There is a pattern of ruthless determinism in the natural behaviour of plants and animals. The survival of the individual has no importance compared to the survival of the population. An organism does nothing but serve the

OVERLEAF: CRUMMOCK WATER, CUMBRIA

genes which it carries, while the system of genetic mutation ensures the death of many individuals before they mature and give birth themselves. It is a policy of severe frontiersmanship, where the central deciding authority of population-survival pushes many individuals beyond the edge of known survivability in the hope that one in a million will found a new colony. The others are necessary wastage.

This is an alarming model for human attitudes to the landscape. Nature knows nothing of preservation. It cannot rely on any maintenance of the status quo. It must assume that circumstances are changing and cannot allow itself to be boxed into rigid structures. Over large parts of the landscape many people still assume that this sort of necessity – the natural assumption – is the only force that matters. Farmers in Britain still need no planning permission for buildings under five thousand square feet, if they are a certain distance from roads or housing. Land use, except in a few special areas, is totally unrestricted. Even those Sites of Special Scientific Interest, which preserve particular botanical or ornithological environments, are frail things when set against the resolution of the modern farmer, for whom growth – economic growth – remains a shibboleth. A drained wetland or a ploughed moor cannot return to its previous state simply by being left alone. Even with the recent legislation that compensates farmers who agree not to improve sensitive areas, the destruction of many fragile habitats still occurs. There is still a respect in some quarters for the 'realism' of the farmer's attitude, compared with the pastoralism, the literariness, even the sentimentality of the conservationists.

The present debate over the future of the countryside is the meeting of these two attitudes, one imbued with the idea that the landscape is a process in which men must react to circumstances to survive and where nothing must be allowed to interfere with the alertness of that reaction; and the other sees the landscape as a treasured object, a historical document and a reservoir of Englishness which current greed must not be allowed to erase. Thirty thousand acres of Britain are now covered by motorway and the

RUMPS POINT, NEAR POLZEATH, NORTH CORNWALL

BUTTERMERE, CUMBRIA

LOCH TULLA, STRATHCLYDE, SCOTLAND

When the lochs are still they are at their most powerful.

BLACK ROCK COTTAGE, GLENCOE, SCOTLAND

TOWARDS TRYFAN, SNOWDONIA, WALES

BENN DORAIN AT AUCH, STRATHCLYDE,
SCOTLAND

LOCH TUATH, ISLE OF MULL

ST MARY'S LOCH, THE BORDERS, SCOTLAND

*Only two hours before, the reeds were shaken by
a violent storm.*

National Trust has over a million members. Fifty thousand acres of farmland disappear each year under suburban and industrial development, an area the size of Berkshire once every five years, while two out of every five people take a country walk at least once a week. London merchants used to escape to smog-free country cottages in the seventeenth century and disgust at the polluted air of the capital was expressed a hundred years before that, but these old attitudes have reached a new pitch in this century. The extremes of commercial necessity and a belief in the rural view – heavily interdependent as they are – are further apart than ever before.

If we expand the idea of *necessity*, there may be a way of reconciling these contradictory extremes. If necessity can take in spiritual satisfaction as well as economic well-being, then the rural landscape will have more of a chance. It will be possible, for example, to look after the varieties of the countryside rather than to subsidise farmers for the over-production of barley and milk at the expense of rural monotony. It will be possible to invest, for example, in the particular 'hereness' of a place rather than in its productivity. This may create fantasy-zones, but in the particularities of a valley or a wood it is certainly as possible to suspend disbelief as in a theatre, a cinema or a book. Educationalists say that Britain, with much of the western world, is moving into a 'post-literate phase'. The dominance of the word since the Renaissance is undermined, they say, by the fluid visibility of modern culture. If this process is really happening, it becomes even more urgent to ensure a stability – not an immobility – in the rural landscape. At bottom, that landscape is a geometry. It provides a language beyond words in which a post-literate culture could always find value and meaning on a subtle scale. Some of these things can of course be found in some urban landscapes too, but there is a particularly permanent reality – independent of men – in the countryside, a sort of grammar that makes a stream different from a brook, a rivulet, a tributary, a trickle and a river. When any or all of them are channelled into a one-sized drain, the meaning begins to go.

TOWARDS BEN NEVIS, THE HIGHLANDS, SCOTLAND

LINDISFARNE, NORTHUMBERLAND

In a spartan landscape, nothing is wasted, and an old boat has been converted into three, presumably watertight, sheds.

CRAG LOCH, HADRIAN'S WALL, NORTHUMBERLAND

ALUM BAY, ISLE OF WIGHT

ERME MOUTH, DEVON

Charlie Waite's photographs are framed in this language. He is English and the photographs are all of places in Britain. Nevertheless, they often recreate the universal language of the landscape itself, unaware of nationality and dependent only on the detailed patterning of its elements. There is a supremacy in nature of quality over quantity, and of shape over stuff. It can be no coincidence that a tree, a nerve cell and a river-system all branch in a similar way, nor that the random pressure of bees' bodies in wax and random contractions in basalt as it cools produce the same hexagonal grid. When, as Charlie says, 'the camera becomes no more than a channel, along which I and the landscape can pass,' he is doing nothing more or less than joining the pattern and finding the resonance. Because pattern and appearance matter more than anything else in the landscape it is easy to make this connection across enormous physical divides. Our mind is part of the structure. In the landscape we can recognise ourselves as part of it and it as part of ourselves. As the poet and painter Kenneth Rexroth has said:

Under this tree for a moment,
We have escaped the bitterness
Of love, and love lost, and love
Betrayed. And what might have been
And what might be, fall equally
Away with what is, and leave
Only these ideograms
Printed on the immortal
Hydrocarbons of flesh and stone.

GOSPEL PASS, GWENT, WALES

STOB DEARG, AT THE HEAD OF GLENCOE

GLENCOE, THE HIGHLANDS, SCOTLAND

If landscapes were sold, like sheets of
characters of my boyhood, one penny plain
and twopence coloured, I should go to the
length of twopence every day of my life.

Robert Louis Stevenson

JAN 1 7 2024